No More Secrets
Expose the Family Predators

Don't Touch Me

Jennifer & Taron 'Juju' Boston

To My Baby Girl,

Mommy sincerely apologizes that someone we trusted took advantage of you in the worst possible way. Thank you for sharing your experience and trusting me. I'm confident that with God, you will heal… We will heal, and you will lead an abundant, fulfilling life.

You are my hero!

Love always,
Mom

To every person that was violated and dismissed, denied an opportunity for justice and support, I send you love and light.
I believe you.
I support you.
I stand with you.

I laid across the bed after a long day of play.

He came into the room and took my innocence away.

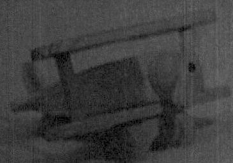

He touched me in a way that didn't feel right.

I wondered why it was happening. Why wasn't there anyone else in sight?

I laid there still. No words were exchanged.

Slowly but surely, my mind drifted away.

I thought back to the time when it seemed that he cared.

When he protected us all, and we had no reason to be scared.

Yet here I was, wanting to scream but unable to speak.

I wished someone would bust into the room and stop this from happening to me.

After what seemed like forever, he got up and left.

I hurriedly pulled up my clothes, gasping for breath.

Finally, someone came in and I asked for help.

She left to go tell a responsible adult.

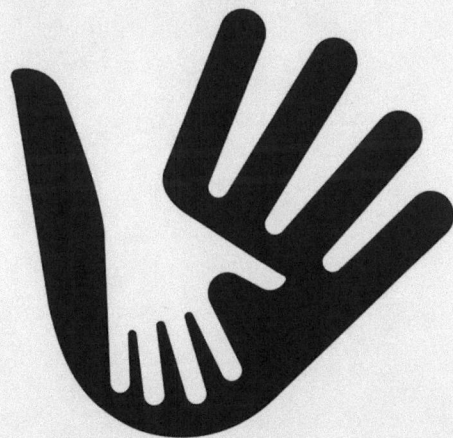

The adult looked at me strangely as I recalled the truth.

She stood motionless, slightly smiling—no sympathy, just aloof.

My gut told me something wasn't right, which was proven right after. She went and got the monster, who denied the whole thing.

Made me apologize and promise not to tell my dad, which I couldn't believe!

SILENCE

Everything was a blur for a while thereafter.

Until I told my mom a "joke" that didn't end in laughter.

Mom said, "That's a bad joke. Please don't repeat it again.

"If anyone is ever to touch you,

tell me ASAP,

I mean it,

the end!"

I told mom what happened. She was instantly filled with rage.

She jumped into action, saying everyone will pay!

She called the cops, the district attorney, and a therapist too.

She said, "We will make it through this. You're victorious. There's a warrior that lives inside you!"

BRAVE

Mom assured me I did nothing wrong and thanked me for being brave.

She apologized that I wasn't protected by those who should have kept me safe— adults that should know how to behave.

Since telling my mom, several things happened.

Many people came forward and shared their ordeal with an attacker.

They thanked me for helping to set them free.

Said they carried their secret so long, they didn't know what they'd do without me.

COURAGE

I was still a little nervous about sharing my story, didn't want to be judged, but I stayed strong.

Mom assured me I had nothing to be embarrassed about; I had done nothing wrong.

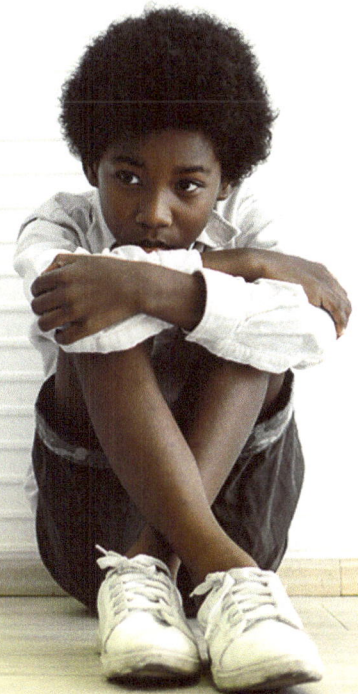

I am here today to encourage you all.

Don't be scared or shy. Point them out, make them fall!

Adults should protect us, not make us feel scared.

They definitely shouldn't touch and then threaten to tear us to shreds.

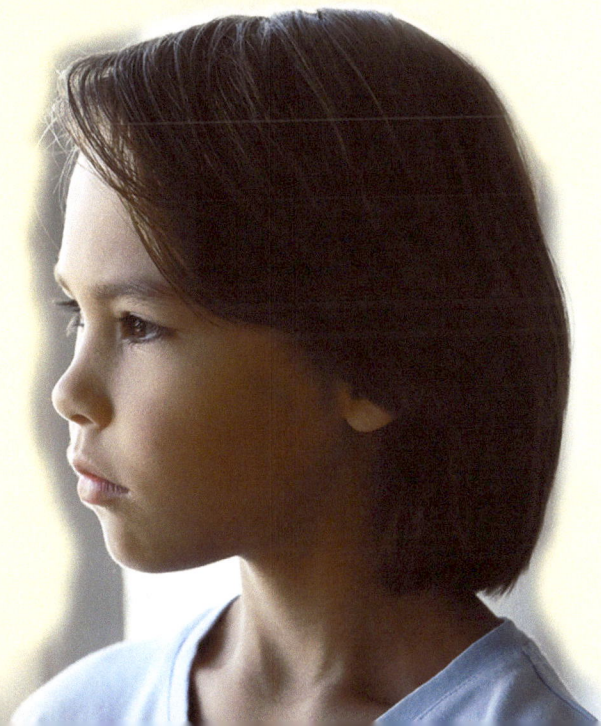

No one should take advantage
because they can.

We are innocent children. Why is this
anyone's plan?

If you decide not to listen to anything else I have to say:

Please just consider this, don't further delay!

If anyone ever touched you in a not-so-nice way:

It's time to be courageous. Go tell someone today!

If they don't believe you,
tell someone else.
You deserve to be loved, respected,
and protected, even if it has to start
with yourself.

A Word from the Authors

No one has a right to touch your body, speak to you inappropriately, or make you feel uncomfortable by saying things about your body that you do not like.

Do not let anyone make you feel bad about something they did to you. You are not a bad child. You are not 'fast,' possessed, and no, you did not want it.

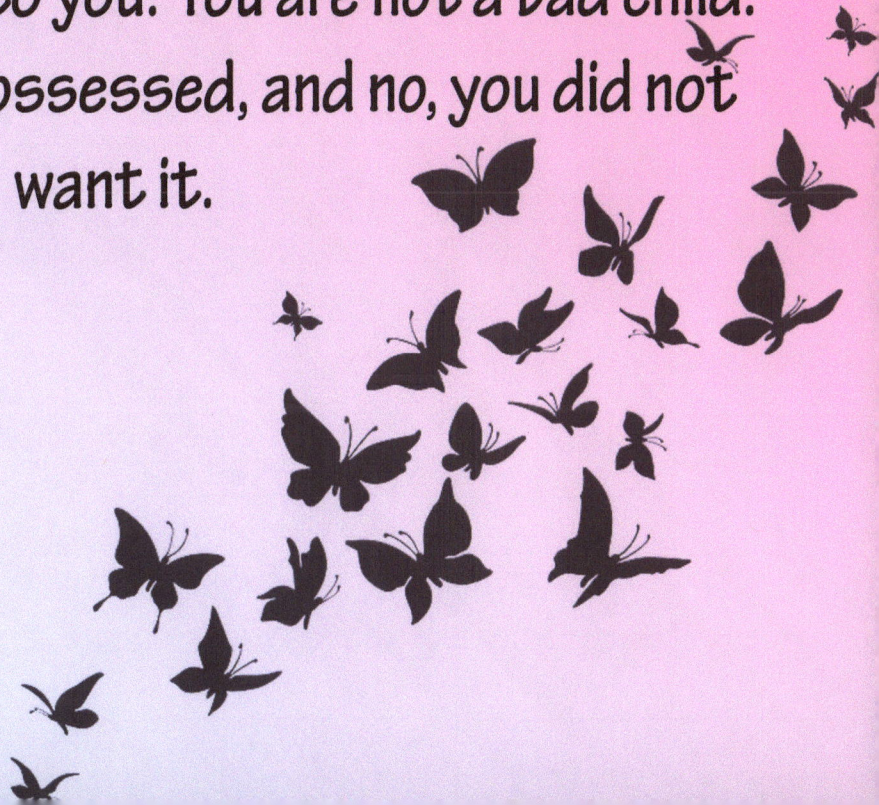

A Word from the Authors

There is no shame or embarrassment in what happened to you. The only Person that should be both ashamed and embarrassed is the monster that hurt you.

You deserve to be believed, protected, and loved.

A Word from the Authors

Speak up! If you see something, say something!

If you are scared to tell the adults in your home, tell an adult that doesn't live in your home—such as an adult at school, a place of worship, afterschool or weekend activity. You can even tell the police.

A Word from the Authors

If you tell an adult and they don't believe you, tell another adult. Keep telling adults until someone does something to help and protect you. You can even tell a friend and ask them to tell their parent(s) or guardian(s).

Don't believe them when they tell you they will hurt, kill, or harm you or anyone else. In the moment, tell them anything they want to hear to keep yourself safe from further harm and then as soon as you can, tell an adult.

About the Authors

Jennifer Boston was born and raised in the projects of NYC. A high school dropout at age 15, she received her GED from Job Corps at the tender age of 16. By the age of 20, she joined the United States Army, where she acquired a new outlook on life. A single mom by the age of 22, she left the military and later returned to school. Within 5 years, she earned an associate's, bachelor's, and master's degree with honors. In 2017, she self-published her first children's book, "Juju 'Round The World" in five languages, which takes you on the journey of relocating her family from Atlanta, GA, to Japan for her new career post-college from her daughter's perspective. They enjoyed living in Japan and Germany, which afforded them the opportunity to travel abroad to several countries throughout Asia, Europe, and Africa.

Currently residing in Cuba, she enjoys giving back to communities globally, while encouraging everyone she encounters to "live their best life" despite their circumstances. She believes in the power of positive affirmations #IAM

Taron "Juju" Boston is 10 years old and enjoys life abroad. Courageous and adventurous, Juju can be found jumping in the pool with friends, making all of the new TikTok videos, and inventing her own fashion trends.